HERO

Pirate
Gold

Steve Barlow and Steve Skidmore

Illustrated by Sonia Leong

D1149021

FRANI

LONI

First published in 2008
by Franklin Watts

Text © Steve Barlow and Steve Skidmore 2008
Illustrations © Sonia Leong 2008
Cover design by Jonathan Hair

Franklin Watts
338 Euston Road
London NW1 3BH

Franklin Watts Australia
Level 17/207 Kent Street
Sydney, NSW 2000

ISBN: 978 0 7496 8264 4

1 3 5 7 9 10 8 6 4 2

Printed in Great Britain

Franklin Watts is a division of Hachette Children's Books,
an Hachette Livre UK company.
www.hachettelivre.co.uk

Decide your own destiny...

This book is not like others you may have read. *You* are the hero of this adventure. It is up to you to make decisions that will affect how the adventure unfolds.

Each section of this book is numbered. At the end of most sections, you will have to make a choice. The choice you make will take you to a different section of the book.

Some of your choices will help you to complete the adventure successfully. But choose carefully, some of your decisions could be fatal!

If you fail, then start the adventure again and learn from your mistake.

If you choose correctly you will succeed in your adventure.

Don't be a zero, be a hero!

You are an English adventurer in the reign of Queen Elizabeth I.

Ever since Elizabeth became Queen, King Philip II of Spain has been looking for an excuse to invade England. Elizabeth and her navy are too weak to challenge the power of Spain directly; so the Queen secretly employs 'privateers' or 'gentleman pirates' to attack Spanish ships.

The bravest and most successful of these privateers is Francis Drake. He is so feared by the Spanish that they call him 'El Draco' – 'The Dragon'.

You set sail with Drake and his brother John from Plymouth in May 1572 with two ships, the *Pasha*, and the *Swan*, and 73 volunteers.

After several weeks crossing the Atlantic Ocean, you arrive on the Spanish Main (the Caribbean) and land at the secret harbour of Port Plenty, discovered by Drake on his earlier voyages. Now you are about to strike your first blow against the Spanish with an attack on the harbour of Nombre de Dios.

Now turn to section 1.

1

Drake calls you and the men together. "Our task is to steal the gold and silver being sent back to Spain from the mines in Peru, so that it can be used to strengthen our beloved England against Spanish attack. Some of this gold and silver has already been brought to the harbour. It is being kept in the Spanish Governor's house.

"We will attack in three small boats. I will command the first boat." Drake points at you. "I want you to be in charge of the second boat." You nod in agreement. "We will attack tonight under cover of darkness."

That evening you glide into the Spanish harbour with your sails down and your oars muffled.

Suddenly, there is a cry from a watchtower overlooking the harbour. A moment later, bells ring in the churches of the town. Your boats have been spotted, and you no longer have the element of surprise.

If you wish to continue with the attack, go to 31.

If you wish to stop the attack and turn your boat around, go to 15.

2

That night, as you are standing at the ship's rail, you hear movement behind you in the darkness. Before you can turn, strong hands grab you by the heels and shoulders, and tip you overboard.

You hit the water with hardly a splash. As you surface, gasping for breath, you see that the ship has sailed on. Nobody hears your cries. Soon you will drown – if the sharks don't find you first.

Your adventure is over. If you wish to begin again, turn back to 1.

3

"That ship is too strong for us at present," you tell your men. "We'll follow her, and force her to go to the West of Cuba. That will give us more time and put us both in shallow water, where a small ship like ours will have an advantage."

But as the days pass, your men become restless. Eventually, one man, Robert Pike, steps forward. "Some of the lads want to go back to

Port Plenty," he says bluntly. "We think this is a fool's errand."

Your authority is being challenged. This is mutiny!

If you agree to turn back, go to 16.

If you want to order your men to arrest Pike, go to 43.

4

"I knew I could count on you," says Drake.

He shows you a chart of the Caribbean Sea. "You must catch the galleon in the harbour of Nombre de Dios if you can. If not, you must prevent her from meeting up with the Spanish treasure fleet at Havana on the island of Cuba. If that happens, there will be too many ships for you to fight."

Pedro speaks up. "Half of my men will go with Capitán Drake. I and the others will join your crew – if you will accept us."

Pedro's men are not sailors – they might be more trouble than they are worth.

If you decide to accept Pedro's help, go to 33.
If you decide to refuse it, go to 9.

5

The Spanish captain panics. He thinks that your sudden attack and signals must mean that other English ships are nearby.

The galleon turns away from you. A short while later, it runs aground in the shallow water between the Bahama Islands. Masts and rigging break and the ship keels over, stuck fast. The galleon is at your mercy.

If you decide to open fire on the stricken galleon, go to 22.

If you decide to send boats to demand the Spaniards surrender, go to 34.

6

The fresh Spanish troops attack. Your men are carrying heavy bags and bars of gold and silver, and cannot defend themselves. Many are killed or wounded.

Realising that the position is hopeless, you order your men to drop the treasure they are carrying and make a dash for the boats.

Go to 11.

7

You order Pike to be hanged from the yardarm. He is hauled off the deck, legs twitching. When he stops kicking, he is cut down and thrown overboard.

Pike's friends are very unhappy. They mutter amongst themselves, plotting your downfall.

Go to 2.

8

You arrive safely back at Port Plenty, but you have brought back very little and more bad news awaits.

While you have been away, Francis Drake's

brother, John, took the *Swan* out to sea and was killed trying to capture a much larger and better-armed Spanish ship.

"God rest his soul," says Captain Drake.

Some days later, Drake sends for you. "Pedro tells me that a Spanish galleon has arrived in Nombre de Dios to load gold and silver," Drake says. "He has also told me of a mule train that is about to bring more gold and silver across from Panama City. I shall attack the mule train. I want you to take John's place as captain of the *Swan* and capture the galleon."

If you accept the command, go to 4.
If you refuse the command, go to 17.

9

You tell Pedro that you can't use his men. He scowls. Drake looks doubtful but says nothing. Later, as you are checking stores for the *Swan*, Pedro and his friends appear. Some are armed and are shouting threats.

Fearing for your life, you order your men to open fire on them. Pedro and his friends are killed.

Go to 24.

10

The missing sailor's friends ask you to search for him.

"I'm sorry, men," you tell them, "but even if he survived the fall and isn't drowned yet, there's no chance of finding him on a moonless night and in such a sea. And if we stay, we'll lose the galleon. We all knew the risks when we signed up for the voyage."

The men shake their heads, but do not argue. You now have to decide what to do if you succeed in overtaking the galleon: will you fight, or try cunning first?

If you decide to fight, go to 32.

If you decide to try to fool the Spanish captain, go to 49.

11

Captain Drake is angry. "Only a fool fights against overwhelming odds!" he rages. "Your stupidity has left us with too few men to attack the Spanish. We have no choice but to rejoin our ships and set sail for England, empty-handed."

You have failed. If you wish to begin the adventure again, turn back to 1.

12

You call all hands to make sail. The wind begins to rise, but if you take in your sails for safety, you will lose too much speed. Soon the *Swan* is crashing through the waves, and the masts and rigging are groaning with the strain.

Suddenly there is a terrible cracking noise, and the top of the foremast snaps. The lookout in the foretop is thrown into the sea.

You know that the man cannot swim and may already have been killed by the fall.

If you decide to stop and search for the man, go to 23.

If you decide to leave him to drown and press on, go to 10.

13

"Pedro," you say, "ask them what ship is that leaving the harbour? If they do not tell me at once, they will die."

Pedro translates your threat into Spanish. This angers the fishermen, who are not defenceless.

Their leader picks up a trident – a vicious,

three-pronged fishing spear — and hurls it. You feel the cruel points pierce your throat. Your mouth fills with blood and you tumble into the sea. Your bullying has been your undoing.

You are no hero. If you wish to begin again, turn back to 1.

14

You steer towards the Spanish ship, and fire your forward guns. The galleon returns fire. You order one of your men to fly a series of signal flags.

"But who are we signalling to?" he asks.

"The English ships that are coming to join our attack," you tell him.

"But there aren't any English ships coming to join our attack!"

"The Spanish captain doesn't know that. I'm hoping he'll panic."

Now you have to decide on your next move.

If you want to press on with the attack on the galleon, go to 5.

If you decide to pretend to flee, go to 18.

15

You order your men to stop the attack and row back out to sea.

You wait for the other two boats. It is not long before they join you. They are full of injured men. The attack has failed.

Drake is furious. "You traitor!" he shouts at you from his boat. "Your cowardice has cost us victory. I'll see you hanged for this."

Your adventure is over. If you wish to start again, turn back to 1.

16

"Very well," you say. "The ship is too big for us to attack, anyway."

Some of Drake's most trusted men raise a mutter at this, but you order them to be silent. Even so, for the rest of the day you are aware of growing discontent at your decision.

Go to 2.

17

"I am no coward, Captain," you tell him, "but I have never commanded a ship before."

"Let me be the judge of when a man is ready for command," says Drake. "You did well in the attack on the harbour. I say you are ready."

You take a deep breath. "In that case, Captain, I accept."

Go to 4.

18

You turn away from the galleon, which sails on without altering course, ignoring your signals. The Spanish captain knows that you would attack if there were more English ships coming.

In desperation, you turn and attack. But it is too late to fool the Spanish captain. He is ready for you.

Go to 35.

19

You order two men to take Captain Drake back to the boats. As the Spanish guards retreat, you lead a group of men to the Governor's house. Breaking into the strongroom, you find bars of gold and silver.

You order your men to carry these back to the boats. But as you step outside, you hear heavy fighting. More Spanish soldiers have arrived.

If you decide to order your men to continue taking the gold and silver, go to 6.

If you decide to fight off the new troops, go to 41.

If you order your men to drop the treasure and retreat, go to 37.

20

A grating is taken from one of the hatches. You order Pike to be tied to it and lashed with a cat o' nine tails. When you order him to be cut down he is unconscious, his back red with blood.

Go to 2.

21

You order your men to row the prisoners over to the *Swan* while you supervise bringing the gold and silver up from the galleon's hold. But shortly after the last prisoners have gone across, you hear cries and the noise of battle.

Horrified, you look across the water. The prisoners have overwhelmed your crew and taken the *Swan*. Its guns are now aimed at you. The tables are turned. With success within your grasp, you have failed.

If you wish to begin the adventure again, turn back to 1.

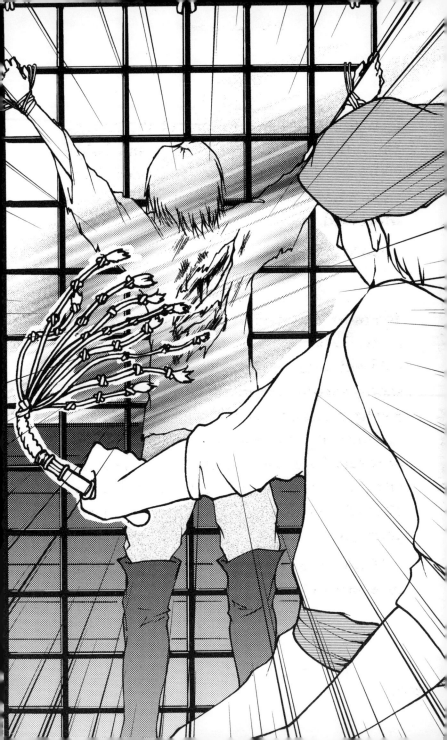

22

You give the order to open fire. The Spanish sailors are helpless. They are cut down by the onslaught until blood flows from the scuppers and streaks the side of the wrecked ship.

But then, one of your shots hits the galleon's store of gunpowder. There is a huge explosion. When the smoke clears, you see that the ship has been blown to pieces.

"How are we supposed to get the treasure now?" asks one of your men.

He is right. The gold has been scattered far and wide on the seabed. Your cruelty has wrecked the mission.

You have failed. If you wish to begin the adventure again, turn back to 1.

23

You call all hands to take in sail and turn the ship. But in the darkness and crashing waves, it is impossible to find the missing man in the water. You give up the search and turn once again to follow the galleon – but you have lost time, and you can no longer see it.

Go to 28.

24

Drake is furious when he hears of your cruelty to the slaves.

"Those men could have helped us," he cries. "You have murdered them for no good reason. You will be sent back to England in chains for your crime!"

You are in disgrace. Your adventure has ended. If you wish to start again, turn back to 1.

25

After a chase lasting many hours, you catch up with the galleon. It is much bigger and more heavily armed than the *Swan*, and you know it will have many more men aboard.

Your orders are to prevent it from joining the rest of the Spanish fleet in Havana. Now you have to decide the best way of doing this.

If you decide to board the ship and fight hand-to-hand for her, go to 48.

If you decide to fight the ship with your cannons, go to 35.

If you decide to follow the ship and wait for a better time to attack, go to 3.

26

Throwing off your ship's disguise, you follow the Spanish galleon through the Florida Straits. You are running out of food and water. Once the galleon reaches the open sea, it will be easy for it to give you the slip.

The coast of Florida is on your left and the Bahama Islands to your right. Should you now attempt to fight the galleon, or try one last trick?

If you decide to fight, go to 35.

If you decide to trick the Spanish captain, go to 14.

27

"Very well," you say, "come with us." The runaway slaves follow you into the boats. Your men row away from the shore and meet up with Captain Drake.

The leader of the ex-slaves is called Pedro. He explains that he and his men were captured by the Spanish in Africa and brought to work in the Americas. Captain Drake is delighted. "These men are just the allies we need. They know the country, and can tell us what the Spanish are up to."

You raise the sails and set course for your base at Port Plenty.

Go to 8.

28

At daybreak, you see to your horror that the galleon has increased its lead overnight. You make more sail in an attempt to catch up, but as dusk approaches, the galleon enters Havana harbour. You cannot follow it under the guns of the Spanish forts protecting the treasure fleet. You will have to turn back to Port Plenty.

You have failed. If you wish to begin the adventure again, turn back to 1.

29

Slowly, you begin to catch up with the Spanish ship. You are very worried. If this is the wrong ship, the treasure galleon will have seen you give chase and try to escape. Your chances of finding it will be very small.

But as you get nearer, Pedro points. "I've seen that ship before, Capitán. It's the treasure ship, all right."

You are very relieved. Your gamble has paid off.

Go to 25.

30

You order your men to bring the gold and silver up from the hold and begin loading it into the boats. But while your attention is on this task, the Spanish prisoners rebel. Your men are quickly overwhelmed.

The Spanish captain gives you a cold smile. "You have lost, Englishman! My men will take your boats and capture your little ship. I am no longer your prisoner – you are mine!"

Your shoulders slump. You have failed at the last hurdle.

Your adventure is over. If you wish to begin again, turn back to 1.

31

You order your men to row hard for the beach. The boat's hull scrapes on sand and shell and you leap out. You lead your men in a charge up the beach through a hail of musket fire from Spanish guards who have come from their barracks to defend the town.

You hear a cry of pain. You see Captain Drake fall, clutching his leg.

If you decide to call off the attack, go to 15.
If you decide to rescue Drake, go to 19.

32

At first light, you find that you have indeed overtaken the galleon. You order the crew to quarters, ready for action.

As the Spanish ship comes within range, you order your gun crews to open fire!

Go to 35.

33

"Thank you, Pedro," you say. "Your men's help will be very valuable."

Pedro smiles grimly. "The Spanish made us slaves. We will fight them any way we can."

A boat rows you over to the *Swan*. You ask the bosun whether the ship is ready to sail.

"I'm sorry, Captain," he says, "We're still loading supplies."

You know that you cannot remain at sea for long without food and water, and you can't fight without gunpowder and shot, but time is short.

If you want to complete loading the stores, go to 42.

If you decide to set off at once, go to 36.

34

You row into the shallows and demand that the galleon surrender to you. The Spanish captain bows. He has no choice.

The galleon has a much bigger crew than yours. You must decide what to do with the prisoners while you take the gold and silver from the hold and transfer it to the *Swan*.

If you want to leave the prisoners on board the galleon, go to 30.

If you want to take them on board the *Swan*, go to 21.

If you decide to send them to a nearby island, go to 44.

35

You fire your forward guns, but most of your shots fall short and splash into the water. The Spanish ship has bigger guns and opens fire. The shots tear into your ship. Splinters fill the air. Ropes and blocks from the rigging fall around you. Your sails hang in tatters. The *Swan* is beginning to sink.

Before you can order the men to abandon ship, you feel a sharp pain as a Spanish musket ball rips through your body. Blood pours from your chest and you drop to the deck before blackness engulfs you.

You have failed. If you wish to begin the adventure again, turn back to 1.

36

"We've no time to waste!" you cry. "We'll have to leave the rest of the supplies. Set sail at once!" You sail to Nombre de Dios, but find the Spanish ship is too well guarded for you to risk an attack with your boats, and you do not have enough powder and shot to fight with your ship's guns.

You have no choice but to go back to Port Plenty and complete loading your stores.

Go to 42.

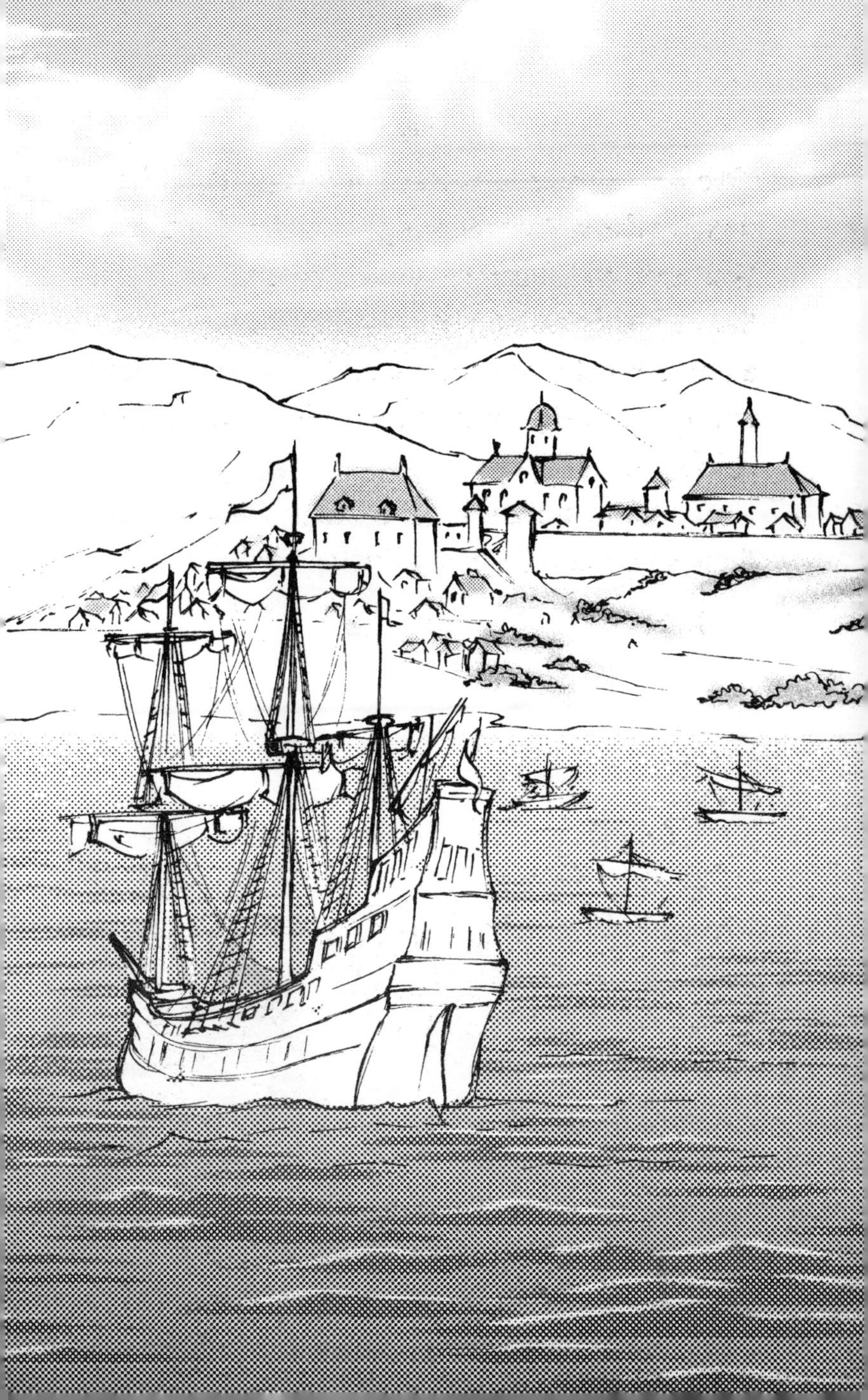

37

You tell your men to retreat in good order. Those with muskets provide covering fire. Your men's swords and axes clear a path to your boats. Just as you are about to launch your boat, a group of men in rags appears from the trees. They are neither Spanish nor Indian, but black. One of the men steps forward. "Amigo, we were slaves. We have run away from the Spanish. Take us with you. We will help you fight!"

You cannot be sure that the man is telling you the truth. Is this a Spanish trap?

If you decide to trust him, go to 27.
If you think it is a trap, go to 45.

38

As soon as they understand that you are offering a fair price for their catch, the fishermen are friendly. With Pedro translating, they tell you that the ship that has just left is indeed the treasure galleon, bound for Havana. You thank them and return to the *Swan*, pleased with your success. Now you know for certain that you are on the track of the Spanish gold – and your crew have fresh fish to eat!

Go to 25.

39

You tell Pedro what to say.

"Send a boat if you wish," he calls, "but I warn you, we have yellow fever aboard. Havana is full of it!"

The Spanish captain curses. He doesn't want the deadly fever on his galleon. He turns away from your ship – and from Havana! Your trick has worked.

You follow, keeping the galleon's sails just in sight.

Go to 26.

40

"Pike," you say, "you are a good seaman. I could hang you for mutiny: but if we're to take that galleon, I shall need every man. Just make sure you do your duty in future, and remember that there can only be one captain on this ship."

Pike touches his forehead in salute. "Aye aye. Thank you, sir."

Go to 46.

41

You charge the new Spanish troops, but there are too many of them. Despite fighting bravely, some of your men are cut down.

You realise that if you try to fight any longer, your force will be wiped out. You order your men to retreat to the boats.

Go to 37.

42

As soon as the stores are loaded, you set sail. But as you approach Nombre de Dios, you see a ship leaving. Is it the treasure ship, or a different vessel?

If you decide it must be the treasure ship and wish to give chase at once, go to 29.

If you decide to check which ship it is, go to 47.

43

Your men step forward and seize Pike. His friends mutter, but when your men put their hands to their swords, they fall silent.

As captain, you have the right to try Pike. It is an open and shut case of mutiny. You find Pike guilty. Now you must pass sentence.

If you decide to hang Pike, go to 7.

If you decide to have him lashed at the grating, go to 20.

If you decide to release him with a warning, go to 40.

44

You leave the Spanish crew on the nearby island of No-name Kay with food and water from their own supplies. You take three Spanish prisoners to help you load the gold and silver: later, you send them to Havana in a boat to tell the Spanish authorities to pick up the stranded prisoners.

You return to Port Plenty with the captured treasure. Then you go to meet Captain Drake. He has successfully intercepted the Spanish mule train and captured more gold and silver than he can carry. He is delighted by your success.

"Come," he tells you, "climb this tree with me." Puzzled, you climb. From the topmost branches, you see a line of shimmering blue water.

"That is the Pacific Ocean," Drake tells you. "No Englishman has ever sailed those waters. But I shall, and you will sail with me. But first we must return home."

Go to 50.

45

"Liar!" you cry. "You are Spanish spies. Kill them, men!"

Your men obey and soon the helpless slaves lie dead on the sand.

You board your boat and return to Port Plenty.

Go to 24.

46

The *Swan* is very close behind the galleon now. The coast of Cuba is on your left, the deadly shallows of the Great Bahama Bank to your right.

As darkness falls, you have a decision to make. You can continue to follow the galleon, or make more sail. This is risky: in the darkness, you may run aground and wreck your ship. But if you are lucky, you may overtake the galleon and head it off before it reaches Havana.

If you decide to continue to follow the galleon, go to 28.

If you decide to try to overtake the galleon, go to 12.

47

You spot a fishing boat casting its nets just offshore. You decide to ask the fishermen whether the ship leaving port is the treasure galleon.

You lower a boat and your men row you across while you consider how to approach the fishermen.

If you decide to threaten them, go to 13.

If you decide to buy their catch and treat them kindly, go to 38.

48

Your hull hits the side of the galleon with a grating crash. You lead your men whooping and yelling onto the galleon's deck.

But the Spanish ship is swarming with heavily armed men. You fight bravely, but your men fall around you one by one. You realise that boarding the galleon was not the right decision. In that moment of despair, the Spanish captain runs you through with his sword.

Your adventure is over. If you wish to start again, turn back to 1.

49

You order your men to disguise the *Swan* as a Spanish ship. The sailmaker sews a Spanish flag and you order the men to paint red crosses on spare sails, which you hoist in place of the usual ones.

By morning, your crew is exhausted. But you have succeeded in overtaking the Spanish ship, and now turn towards it as if you are coming from Havana. Pedro, wearing your captain's coat, hails the Spanish captain.

"If you're looking for the treasure fleet, it sailed yesterday. You'll catch up with it in the Florida Straits if you hurry."

The Spanish captain seems suspicious. He shouts that he is sending a boat across. As soon as it comes closer, he will discover your disguise.

If you decide you now have no choice but to fight, go to 35.

If you decide to try another trick, go to 39.

50

You return to Port Plenty and set sail for home with a hold full of gold and silver. You arrive in Plymouth in August 1573. Boats row out to meet you. Church bells ring in celebration. The forts guarding the harbour fire their guns in salute.

You and Captain Drake travel to London, where you are received by Queen Elizabeth at the Palace of Westminster.

"Your country thanks you," she says. "The gold you have recovered will help to keep England safe from the Spanish king. You are a hero!"

All these I, Hero titles are available now!

Death or Glory!
Steve Barlow - Steve Skidmore
978 0 7496 7664 3

Viking Blood
Steve Barlow - Steve Skidmore
978 0 7496 7665 0

Gorgon's Cave
Steve Barlow - Steve Skidmore
978 0 7496 7666 7

Code Mission
Steve Barlow - Steve Skidmore
978 0 7496 7667 4

Save the Empire!
Steve Barlow - Steve Skidmore
978 0 7496 8265 1

Save the Empire!

Steve Barlow and Steve Skidmore

Illustrated by Sonia Leong

It is September 1851. You are a famous private detective living in London. Whenever the police at Scotland Yard are unable to solve a crime, they always call you to help them.

Queen Victoria is on the throne and the British Empire is the greatest in the world. However, it is a time of great tension between Britain and Russia.

It is also the year of The Great Exhibition. This is designed to display the industrial power of Britain. It has been visited by thousands of people from around the world.

It is almost midnight and you are reading in your rooms, when you hear a knock at the door. You wonder who would be calling at this time of night.

I HERO
DECIDE YOUR OWN DESTINY
Save the Empire!
Steve Barlow - Steve Skidmore